Upon a
Slender Stalk

Larry Grimes

authorHOUSE®

AuthorHouse™
1663 Liberty Drive
Bloomington, IN 47403
www.authorhouse.com
Phone: 833-262-8899

Published by AuthorHouse 01/18/2022

ISBN: 978-1-6655-4806-9 (sc)
ISBN: 978-1-6655-4805-2 (e)

Library of Congress Control Number: 2021925839

Print information available on the last page.

Contents

Dedication

To Carol:
Sunshine on Cloudy Days

Aubade—Bethany WV

My window is open
It is 3:33 in the shriek of owl
in the hoo-hoot of the second owl

The sky is cloud
There is no moon
The river runs high and fast
Above the burble of rocks

Cicadas do not rub their legs
The frogs are silent
No coyote howl. No raccoon snarl.
No deer snort. Only the white noise of night.

Then, at first light, robin song
cardinal whistle, sparrow chirp
coffee smell and
the sharp cut of crisp air
when I walk out the door

3:00 am (near Mancos CO)

That hour
o'clock
in the soul

a window
full moon

dark objects
in the meadow

black dots
moving toward me

one 20 feet away
feeding on tall grass

others recede into a grove of pinion and cedar
great white rumps move away

the pane dissolves
dung smell of elk
deep in my lungs

my eyes haze
I blink
The figures have vanished

the pane returns
the elk remain

3:07 am

In The Morning When
You Have No Words

what do you say to the silence
as you whisk the eggs
with the splash of milk

A pat of butter sizzles
in the hot iron skillet

The eggs have been cracked
so we can make an omelet
mincing garlic, dicing peppers
slicing onions, grating cheese
reaching for words in the morning
to fold gently into the silence

Blue Heron

I look downstream through cataract eyes
and, darkly, see a solitary fisher standing
midstream on a large flat rock.

As quiet as prayer, as still as death.

Then a sudden strike and catch
as wide wings open and lift
the great bird upward and away.

Death Of A Hummingbird

Wing flutter
at the corner of my eye

Wings stall
Bird plummets

A tiny *rufous*
Gasping lungs

My pulse quickens
I breathe hard

Its body convulses
I shake

Then stillness

Not a flutter

Emptiness
a beautiful emerald emptiness
glistens under bright sun

Kingfisher

I have walked my path to the river nine years now
killing the grass in my way, wearing a dirt trail to the bank's edge.
Each day I step to the Watching Stone, christened in a child's game.
There I keep vigil for the Kingfisher. It is here or nowhere I shall find him.

I wait by the yellow water counting ice-slabs, tires, and tree trunks in the
swirl
For he is sometimes seen in free-fall at late day against the winter sun.

I have not missed a day or seen a feather against the changing sky, but
he is known to flash blue, to plunge-fall in Easter dawn at silent prey.

I stand mid-day, silent on the mud bank—less now a sand grain, and
eddy's swirl—for he is a summer's bird, a silver ingot shrieking from
sun-center screaming down the day.

I who still watch, watch still in the hoar frost on the stone slab.
May he come as grey-blue fire against the first fall frost, fire on the
diamond water.
I have walked my path to the river ten years now,
killing the grass in my way, wearing a dirt trail to the bank's edge.
Each day I step to the Watching Stone, christened in a child's game.
There I keep vigil for the Kingfisher. It is here or nowhere I shall find him.
For here is the trail's end, the Watching Stone and the prey.

Two Longs and a Snort

I biked slowly above Castleman's Run
The water a quiet murmur over the rocks
It is dry season now and the rush is gone

In the woods on my left a deer snorts three times
The snorts echo my father's grand sneezes
Two long snorts, one short one

It mirrors long ago rings of our wall phone
The snorts a code I hear through echo,
know in reflection
but cannot crack

So I say "Bless you" and pedal on
toward the high bluff where
kingfishes plunge from sun to water

Celtic Love Knot

Black snakes copulating in the sugar maple
Picture that. Sleek blue-black snakes
Twenty feet up, twined
like a Celtic love knot.
Out on a limb. A public proclamation
To us gathered below: "Be fruitful and multiply!"
And so we broke some wheat bread
Raised our glasses,
assembled as we were to party on the deck.
Raised our glasses
and drank deep red gulps.

Beautiful, Beautiful Zion

I zoom the camera all the way out
and see them there on the high cliff
silhouettes, paper figures, Bergman's dancers

They are marching, walking any way, in Zion
beautiful, beautiful Zion—worth a hymn—
the hikers, Zion, the cliff faces, the river

Snow water roars through the canyon
feeding a swamp in the desert
hanging flowers on the walls

Mormons built homes here, and beavers
Utes walked the Narrows before us
And the Ancient Ones left shards

Emerson was right about cathedrals
but his eyes never saw this Salisbury
in Utah, this Notre Dame of uncut stone

Mountains Can Fly

Running the I-8 from El Cajon to Yuma
mountains take flight
hard spiked mountains break the sky in Mexico
turn to gigantic boulder piles along the canyons
become great dunes near El Centro
and float as dust in my nostrils come Yuma
There is replication–
take 160 out of Alamosa
toward Fort Garland
Blanca Peak, Tsisnaasjiní
(Dawn Mountain), granite
crown of the Sangre de Christo,
it grabs the eye, raises
it out of the valley
toward a glare of whiteness

in its shadow sand

piled up in shifting mounds
great dunes sing in the wind
ancient people chip rock

In the dust of sand grains
the smell, the taste, of mountains flying

Alive to Light

Meditation on Psalm 40:9-11

We were climbing slowly
out of the deep
valley under heavy canopy.
It was dark there beneath the trees.
We could feel the valley rise
step by step. Our thighs loosened. The pain left.
The trail flattened and ran a straight course along a ridge.
Then, to our right, we saw it.
Where trees had been the full sky was alive with light.
Stars. Galaxies of stars.
We walked out onto solid rock
stood, stared into the bright.
The moon hung in crescent,
The love star reached down beneath it.
We put our packs down on the rocks
Pulled out a loaf of flat bread, broke it and ate.
Then we slept in the soft glow
waking In crisp dawn looking down into a meadow
Where a young boy carried a lamb in his arms.
Behind him the ewe followed
toward the open door of a barn.

October Song

It's hard to sing a June song in October
to hold copper skin against the orange bittersweet
to play a summer tune on stops blown by autumn wind

Fisher of Fish

The words were clear and whispered
"You shall be a fisher of fish,
of flesh and bone in fast waters."
So I cast in the shadow of fallen rocks
great boulders splitting the current
in quiet pools below spent falls
I catch, touch with wetted hand,
marvel at weight and length and specked glory
then release, gently, again into the flow.

Beyond

that peace
that passes understanding
that rest beyond desire
beyond will
beyond the thingness of things
beyond accumulation, beyond accommodation

Past the thundering cascade
beyond the boulders
waters spread out, shimmer
grow flat and still

A trout breaks water

"Head, Heart, Hands, Health"

4-H Club Pest Drive
Winter 1968

We wrung their necks
soft, light, feathered bodies
sparrow, starling, wren

Ten cents a body
--extra for crows and jays—

Exterminated

With extreme, extreme
prejudice, just like
them in the village

where the body count
was broadcast at six
on CBS news

Sugar Shack

Before he struck the tap
Before the bark was wounded
Before the bucket was hung
Before the sweet water flowed

Dad always paused
Folded his hands
Still holding the mallet
And said:

"Taste and know that God is good."

Then he placed the tap
Drew the mallet back
And said:

"Sorry," before he swung

At each tree it was the same.

Then the water began to drip
I liked it straight from the bucket
Before the boil-down. Mostly water
and the essence of tree. The taste of alive.
Ring after ring of years on the tip of tongue.
Spirit still in it, sliding cool down my throat.

Folks paid for the evaporated water
spirit dissipated water
become sweet, sweet sticky syrup
best thick on pancakes

You couldn't sell the water straight
from the tree. The money was in the stickiness
Long after the words, long after the folded hands
Long after the steam fled the walls of the sugar shack

Randall Fordice: A Threnody

Randall Fordice is a young man with anx old knife
in a land twelve inches deep.
He drives a straight furrow in the late nights
through soil that is not his own.
The seeds will spill another day
The harvest will come another day
His is to plow.

Randall Fordice has dirt in his beard.
He digs graves out of the black earth.
He shaves with an old blade, a straight razor.
Blood soaks his cracked skin and cakes there
where dirt was in his beard.
Randall Fordice digs graves in the flat land.
Holes in the flat land near broken stalks
where pigs root for waste corn.

The black land pales at the second foot.
At six it is red clay.
Randall Fordice rests on his shovel in the grave hole.
Nothing grows from the red clay mud.
The sod is stacked aside.
Randall stares at the shovel blade
scrapes the corners square and ascends.

Mattie Henthorne wore a yellow dress
the day Randall trimmed his beard short.
They stood and pledged it forever

what they had been doing the past two years.
She round bellied in the yellow dress.
That spring he broke ground
and she broke water
the same day.

Randall Fordice swings toward the horizontal
on a small board at the end of two ropes
(furloughed in the early spring).
Two weeks leave
and a rough-hewn pine plank
between him and the pull of gravity.
His arm pulls him back and forth
through a veil of seed pods.
Then his feet plant and drive his body
up to attention.

He wore the olive-drab well that day
and caught me up in his arms.
A big smile bent against my face.
He drooled tobacco juice as he chomped my ear
rough love laced with whiskey breath.
He gnawed and he laughed.

Aloft for real, the Channel becomes land.
The munitions plant, the city, soon under them.
Randall Fordice at his guns. Expolding flames below.
Fourth of July clear.
The children. He knew about the children.
And the women. And the munitions.
And the yellow sulphur flames.

Randall Fordice aimed the flame-thrower at the base of the fence.
He watched the ivy twist dry.
Oily smoke in an upward spiral.
Leaves blacken and crumble.

Poisoned air hung in the fence wire for a moment
as he marched along burning the boundary clear.

The hog, fat under the bristles.
Randall Fordice placed a bullet between its narrow eyes.
The hog lies neck-tight over the rusting tub.
An old knife traces a red line,
scrapes the skin clean as the carcass hangs
split and dripping from a long scald.
Randall Fordice has blood in his beard
as the chittlerins' cook down.
He warms his feet by the oil stove.
The old knife is caked with blood.

Coda:
The Day Bill Vukovich[11] Died.
A car radio blared over the cemetery.
Old Troop Turner's lips
held the shape of taps on cold steel.
His lungs were salt water and the air still.
Grown men stood at parade rest
then fired blank shells into the white sky.
I sat bored and brooding the day Bill Vukovich died.
Brooding as tires whined above commercials
and Randall Fordice screamed, "Hot damn!"
when engines roared into the backstretch.
Pink peonies stood tall in Mason jars.
Foil—gold, blue, silver—gave them glitter in the mid-day sun.
Mom poured tears from the past over the small grave and peonies.
A car radio blared over the cemetery.
Red flags struck the war air
voices moved around the track seeking comment on the fatal turn.

"Randall, Randall Fordice, make the friggin kid turn down the radio.
Ain't you got no respect for the quick nur the dead?"

---

[1] Bill Vukovich—among the greatest Indy 500 drivers. Killed in 1955 pile-up
while in the lead headed for his 3rd straight Indy win.

Ben Hur Nursing Home

Alzheimer's Unit
June 2010

You were asleep when we arrived,
chin on bosom, neck folded left
A collapsed puppet's head.

We wheeled you to a circle of chairs
sat chattering at you
while you continued to sleep

No easy thing
talking against the soft walls of sleep
so Dad applied air to his harmonica

Blew like Joshua, hunting a melody
finding "blood, blood, power in the blood"
he blew against the reeds, "power, power"

"in the blood," you sang
eyes still shut
"in the blood…"

Sis picked it up. Carried it forward.

The Shine of It

Ben Hur Nursing Home
Alzheimer's Unit
2008

It came like water-change,
like current in still deep water
without riffles or rapids

Names stuck at the back of your tongue
words grabbed from the wrong bag
sentences dissolved in their own ink
—the what of intend forgotten

Now you sit beyond the folks who
drool, rock, thump, stare at a TV
with no sound

You choose the corner
by the big fish tank

There your face shapes itself
into a smile
deeper than memory
older than birthdays
grafted to nerve, muscle, bone
a shine in the shadows
toothy, wholesome, vibrant

Tongue unstuck
word grabbed back
sentence unspooled
intend now remanded

Spoken now in the glory of your face
the sheen of our smile

You closed your mouth. Opened your eyes.
Smiled, then sunk again into silence and sleep.

Lamentation and Reprieve

I.
To us, Siamese lovers
joined at the heart,
death comes as surgery
unelected, indelicate--
clumsy handed, amdull instrument trauma—
then a long, long flat-line.

II.
A split-screen
You, seated in your wheel-chair,
I beside you.
Like Job It on my dung-heap
scraping hard with the shards of this life,
scratching at fortune's boils and blisters

You, serene, with a sewing needle in your gnarled hands,
stitch together the pieces of our torn and loving hearts.

The Saint and the Beer Ad

There was a 70s Schlitz beer add
that went like this:
"You only go around once . . .
so go for the gusto"

Isn't very Hindu, but it played in Milwaukee
and Pittsburgh and Boston and Muskogee

You go around once. Then you feed the worms.

Unless, says St. Paul, I tell you a mystery

Still Life—Ostelsheim, Germany

(My wife, Carol's, ancestral village)

Across from the timbered shepherd's house
once home to your grandmother,

Golden against the July sun,
stacked like those in Monet's paintings,
the pile of dung straw smelled of rot
and resurrection

A good six feet high,
not sixteen feet from the west door
of the Dortkirche in Ostelsheim.
I could not see the stable.

Fitzgerald and the Gerasenes

"In the real dark night of the soul it is always three o' clock in the morning, day after day." F. Scott Fitzgerald[2]

When you go there in the night I shall give you pigs
a great herd of pigs to run wild over the edge
words to name each demon, a word to name them all.

Balanced on the edge of sleep, vertiginous on that edge
staring into the void where wild thoughts foam and churn
When you go there in the night I shall send you pigs

Possessed by thoughts you did not think
cannot mouth, thoughts unthinkable
whose barbed edges fish for words
to name each demon
a word to name them all

Thoughts, legion and scattered, beyond command
one foot over the ledge, the other poised to follow
when you stand there in the night I shall send you pigs

Before that step, the word will come
and fill your mouth with the sweet shape of sleep
a word to name each demon, a word to name them all

---

[2] Fitzgerald's comments about 3 am in the soul were made in a 1936 Esquire essay republished in 1945 in Fitzgerald's *The Crack-Up*, edited by Edmund Wilson where it is most accessible today.

Legion, name them Legion, call them forth and name them all
And name them one, Legion, to cast them out into the foaming maw
When you go there in the night I shall give you pigs
and words to name each demon, the word to tame them all.

New Dogs, Old Tricks

It is very hard to teach
Old tricks to new dogs,
Pups full of themselves
Skittering across hard floors,
Clawing to a stop
Leash angry, soiling at will.
And they will—Turkish carpet
Or white shag.
They will not heel
Or toe the line.
Theirs is
to buck-and-wing around the room
Shattering all decorum
and the Waterford vase.

One Book Alone

(with nods to Hemingway and Joyce)[3]

One book alone
ain't got no bloody
fucking chance—
And so I sit, alas, alone.

I'd file for alienation of affection but
that, in you dear reader, would imply attention,
then on, of course, to the passionate sort—

Come on,
Turn a page over, this one or that,
a start of the road to repair.

That's it now,
tickle a pencil along my margins, gently
bend back my spine. I'll fold open to your touch;
I'll spread wide. A little action p-l-e-a-s-e!
Run your fingers down, down lightly
down and across and across and down,
yes, just so, and yes, like that and that

---

[3] My first nod is to James Joyce's *Ulysses*; the last sentences of the novel—Molly Bloom's cascade of "yeses." The second nod is to Ernest Hemingway's *To Have and Have Not* and protagonist Harry Morgan's, hard wisdom—"one man alone ain't got no bloody fucking chance."

We'll both like it, I promise
You and me—we'll begin at the beguine
and come to the end.

So, alienate me no more
Unwrap me, break me open
now, Oh yes, now—and, Oh yes, now.

Red Tag Values

I place on the belt
condoms, salami, vasoline.
The grey cashier faints.

Nude Poetry

We need nude poetry
stripped bare of fashions,
whether vintage or haute couture,
whether from Seattle or Milan
.

Poetry that comes
from a finger in the socket
frizzing the hair,
popping the eyes,
jamming the synapses.

Poetry written on stone tablets
that lives deeper than the self—

Someone, write the I AM again—
vision beyond words,
cracking syllables in two,

spilling IS on the ground
Seed to grow humans again

Blues for Mr. Prufrock[4]

Eat a Peach Blues
Peach got fuzz
and peach got plush
peach got pit
but peach is lush

What I don't know
what they don't teach
is whether that peach
is safe to eat

Tea Time Blues
Her T-shirt says Virginia Woolf
her tea pot whistles Bach
her tea folks come at four each day
but they don't roll and rock

While back and forth the tea folks stroll
Mr. Michael wails the blues
while back and forth the tea folk stroll
that angel blows their dues

Scuttlin' Claw Blues
Hey baby
grab some skin
merry-go horse spin round again

---

[4] A riff on lines from T. S. Elliot's "The Love Song of J. Alfred Prufrock"

yo-yo go up, yo-yo go down
to crack the joke's to be the clown
tide goes out, tide comes in
'direction the crabs go all depends

Trouser Roll Blues
Say sunshine
have you heard
balls lose their bounce and milk won't curd
but steel bends and life gets old
guitars lose their twang, caged bird scolds
and we all end up with our trousers rolled

Peanut Butter Days

Some days I feel crushed
ground, mixed, creamed, blended
sealed in a great shelved jar.

Then you spread me thick
on the fresh, warm
bread of your life
slather me with the sweet
sweet jam of our love

and lift my head to your lips
with a grand, eager smile.

Catch and Release

It is enough
to see the bobble dip

to know you were attached
that you caught my drift

prefectly placed to meet your want

to see the pink of lip on the hook
to know we linked, then you are free

Hydrangeas and Stuffed Shirts

Truant children, we walked in the rain
ambling along the quay at Lake Maggiori
free from the latch of time
hydrangeas as large as sunflowers,
purpled by crayolas, lined the path.

We dash across the street
dance out numbers on the ATM screen
pocket our daily max and

zig and zag from stoop to awning
to doorway. Rain falls gently
as we leap the vacant square
rise above empty tables
past furled umbrellas
then land among the white linen tablecloths
inside burled walnut walls, to be seated
by a starched white shirt.

The whole room turned around the wood fire.
We warmed to its glow, then glowed in our warmth.
"Let him order for us," she said, staring at the starched shirt.
I stacked Euros onto the linen like a high-stakes player.
Bogart-faced, I said, "Something to remember."

Later, and the wine had been good: clean, dry, a touch of almond
blossom.
Later, doors open to the balcony, we lay still

in a tangle of silk, rain tapping snares, a good jazz riff.
You asked, "Can you open the bottle?" I did. With a twist.
You pull a wand from the bottle. Wave it over the chaos.

We blew bubbles through the balcony doors
Across the steeple top and into the purpling sky.

Glass Dancing

The first time I saw you
light danced in a soft breeze
morning dew, web gossamer,
trapping the sun at first flight—
spun glass dancing,
then the flash,
the dazzle of blue eyes

Reckoning Together

You look at me across the table
at the dazzle of dappled sky
crimson, then orange,
blushed down to pink
the sun loses its balance on the ridge
plunges into dusk.
We reckon with the beauty of it

At the Table

The polished circle at which we once sat,
elbow to elbow--sometimes by candle light--
and ate salmon in dill sauce, spinach without complaint,
mussels grilled in white wine and garlic sauce,
that circle was pried apart
extended leaf by leaf,
its surface dulled and scarred.
They spilled oat meal there,
and tales of their days.
Tears, too when hamsters died, or dreams.

The table is extended now,
Stretched to its limit.
Both leaves have been removed.
A great hole gapes in its middle.
Together we push from our opposite directions
toward the center.
In the collapse, a circle forms again,
a golden oak surface on which we place four candles.
A bright flame flickers shadows across the old scars, the new polish.
We sit down quietly together and break the bread.

Mirror, Mirror

Daughter, we danced there once
bowing, twirling
etched in glass.

I looked toward you and our dance
stopped.
From me you spun
raised on toe.
A woman.
Uncanny.

As I stared
every turn of your body was
away.
Out and away
from the mirror
where we once danced,
fixed in glass—

Daughter,
when it is time—
a last dance please.

Saint Valentine's Dance

It is that day again when smart young women wear black,
when befuddled young men assail florists or blush at Victoria's Secret,
when Godiva coats herself in chocolate and begs a tasting,
when Valentine's severed head returns to his shoulders,
when he touches your eyes with saintly hands

And you see the one you love dancing before the mirror
of your remembered lives, dancing to the melody
of desires met, of hopes shared, dancing on into the valley
of the shadow of till-death-do-us part, dancing, dancing
fearing no evil...dancing, dancing on this 14th day of February
in my 78th year—Dancing.

The Ache of It

The ache at the break of it
that sacred vow said so long ago
broken neither by you nor by me

Death did us part
as sure as a surgeon's scalpel
terrible sundering
absolute rending

That joined together so long ago
no longer shows the weld of joining,
though it must be there somewhere
in the wrinkles and sag of flesh
we had become.
Flesh of one flesh,
bones of one bone.
A distinct you and I
Harder each year to discern
—sundered!

The Sea of Prayer

I swim in the sea of prayer
plumbing the deep
in the sea
seeking

My Eyes Sting With the Salt of Tears

My eyes sting with the salt of tears.

O LORD my skin burns and cracks,
take the salt from my tears
make them a seasoning of my faith,
give them the flavor of your steadfast love
that I may taste your grace and
eat from your hand the bread of life.
And the people say, "Amen!"

"Abba! Father!" Amen!

Meditation on Galatians 4:4-7

We've finally been adopted!

Usually they come for the sweet ones,
innocent infants, swaddled and cuddly;
Or the precocious ones: French at three,
piano at four, calculus at six.
Or the sturdy and strong. the very good and kind.

But we have been received,
the whole kit and caboodle of us.
The rag-tag messy mass of us,
all of us as we are.
Right then. Right there. Right now.
Broke the chains that keep us here.
Each and every one of us—child, heir!
Brothers and sisters the time has come!
Shout it out, dance it about,
claim it, name it, cry it aloud:

"Abba! Father!" "Abba! Father!" "Abba! Father!"
                   "Amen!"

A Clod of Earth

Meditation on Psalm 85:8-13

It is good to get dirt under the nails
to mince dark loam between one's fingers
to work the earth with sweating brow.
Who knows what may spring up from the ground?

Keep hoeing, I say. Don't forget faithfulness.
Be sure to water well during a dry spell.
Sit a while in the garden among the lavender.
Chew a mint leaf between your teeth.

Savor the peace that is spoken there.
Hold a lump of dirt in your hand.
Mold it as you were molded.
Breathed into as you were breathed.

A Visitation

One night
I read the New Testament
in a whorehouse in Paw Paw
West Virginia
—to a girl who was a slut—
and who liked it very much
especially Mary who was a virgin
like she was
when she believed in angels.

Minding the Edges

I am mindful of the table edge
As I move the wine glass
Mindful of the bed's edge
As I climb under covers each night
Mindful of the road's edge
As I negotiate the mountain pass
Mindful of the razor's edge
As I shave the curve of my neck
Mindful of edges as I edge to the edge.

Days of Dying and Death

Wednesday—there was dying,
ICU, drugs, tubes. We could
touch and we could pray.

Thursday—Thanksgiving Day.
Mid-morning call. Dead.
Then there was
the blessing to be said
and the meal.

Friday—By appointment, 10 am, the mortician.
Immediate family only.
Obituary, casket, etc., etc., etc.
The pastor spoke no word.

Saturday—Like that ancient one. Nothing.

Sunday—The usual service, of course. Advent.
First Sunday. Hope. Children lit the candle.
Visitation from noon to 4, from 7-9.
Waiting. Watching.

Monday—November 28. False Spring. 70 degrees.
Hundreds of people cancel work. Bright sun. Light rain.
No rainbow was seen. Then there was dinner at the church.

Valley of the Shadow

A terrifying thing, my shadow.
Shape-shifter, Proteus himself.
Me without features,
stretched out like a Dali dream.

When I walk in the valley of the shadow,
helpless hope is my rod and my staff,
hope nevertheless, better than the fear,

I trembled at age three when the shadow was evil.
Much later I wrestled it like Jacob
and brought dark night into my brightest day,
yet I hung on waiting for true night
a victory, a respite, a sleep
before the sun also rose again—
and the shadow

That is how I know death is not evil,
its shadow can be knuckled down.
Hope it seems is not helpless,
nor does hope take the shape of bright sunny days.
It comes in the evening in the gentle dim and ends the day.

After The Crowds

After the crowds disperse
After the cloaks are gathered
After the colt is tethered
After the stones grow silent

After a cloak is stripped
After a back is striped
After the nails pierce
After the body hangs

After the stone rolls away
After fronds are stripped of blades
After a child's hands enfold a cross
Then holy fire consumes all crossed things—

wood and frond and flesh,
grey ash mixed
with blessed water
marks our lives with grace.

Beyond Belief

Believing on a 90-degree day
that ice cream will not melt
is not enough

Agony and Ecstasy

There is no story without the agon
the contest, the contested.
Sure, we can send in the clowns
live happily ever after
bedazzle with epiphany.

But only after the crack
in the mirror, the fly
in the ointment,
only after the villain kicks the dog
only after Pauline's perils,
only after the nail pierces the hand

Like the Needle Stuck

Meditation on Psalm 89:1-18

It is there like the needle
stuck in the groove of a vinyl record—
"Steadfast love, steadfast love. . .
Your faithfulness, Your faithfulness, Your faithfulness"

—round and round and round and over and over and over again
like the seasons, the moon, at Table.
"Steadfast love, Your faithfulness". And not just here
In the holy grove of scripture, but in all Creation

Over and over and over again these words sound
and resound. Above the raging waters, beyond
infinite sparkle of sky, beyond the heavenly multitude.
And here, now, in the daily round and round and round.

From that foundation, from your steadfast love, from your faithfulness
Out spins righteousness and justice with a sound that silences
the babble of the world making happy the people who walk,
who dance in the light of your countenance.

The Meeting of the Bored

Meditation on Isaiah 58:1-12

So, here we sit at the Board Meeting again.
Here we sit bored at meeting again
trying to make these old church bones rise—

Arguing over the color of the carpet,
how to restore the stain-glassed windows,
which sort of music to sing
what our mission statement should be.
Lamentations! Lamentations!

Then the scrape of God fingers run down the blackboard,
Old Isaiah's words pick wax from our ears—a prayer goes up!

God is not with us. God has gone out of our meeting
to meet the shout, to meet the prayer of the oppressed.
Bored with the Board, out God goes forth to
loosen the bonds of injustice,
let the oppressed go free.
Out there, God calls us to walk the talk—
To share bread with the hungry,
bring the homeless poor into our house
to see the naked covered, to be present for our kin.

We who cry for help to make our creaking church bones rise
can get it done, if only we say, "Here I am!"
Stop pointing the finger, stop speaking evil—

if only we offer food to the hungry,
satisfy the needs of the afflicted ...

Then shall our light rise in darkness; our gloom will be like the noonday.
Then the Lord will make our bones strong
and we shall be raised into Kingdom work
and our lives will shout
Glory! Glory! Glory! Glory to the Lord!

Fermenting Joy

It is a gentle ending to the year,
a light snow, a whitening of the trees
the sky a gray veil over the lake

enough snow to fill tire tracks, blot the turkey trail,
erase the edge of things,

and raise questions about the drive to Evensong
where I am to sing the *Magnificat*—
"for he has look-'ed with favor ON
(I like the rise of note here)
his low-o-ly servant"

also chant Psalm 90 with its poignant words
"the span of life is seventy years"
—which I am concluding during these holy days—
"perhaps in strength even eighty"

and so I pray at year's end
knowing that for us all
"years pass quickly and we are gone"

or so it would be if years truly pass
if eternity is naught
if everything must cease
if all is sucked into an abyss we call time

but there is that which is, was, and ever shall be
that which was in the beginning
that which is light and life
that which dark and death cannot diminish

name it light, name it life, name it love
as you wish,
but name it, then call its name

in its name is fruit that grows in winter light
ripens with snow on its skin
fruit that turns to wine on the tongue
fermenting joy in the mouth, and song

a peace settles on it like snow in high country
patience ages both joy and song
a gust of wind wafts kindnesses across the land

it does not end, this wind of kindness
nor the song, not the joy, not patience, nor love
all this comes from an abundance, with a generosity,
that will not be astringed

It is gentle, this presence in the air, hardly a stir
but definitely a force not to be overcome
one can put faith in it—that light breath across the skin

hold fast to it; be disciplined in its way as you look
across the snow field
at the end of this old year

trackless, without horizon
beyond space
and time

It Wasn't Like That

It wasn't like that
A fall? No.
Nothing downward.
Stumble, perhaps,
a lurching, but it was forward,
through the gates

The LORD isn't like that

did not condemn us
who did not know good from evil
until after we made the choice
took the bite, savored the juice,
crushed the pulp between our teeth
and swallowed without dying,
not then
—the serpent did not lie—

but there were consequences
generous, merciful consequences—
there was knowledge of good and evil

a moral sense, options, choices
freedom to give and take, to love and leave
to lose and win, to shout and be silent
to obey and rebel, to ascent and to reject
to serve and to rule, to cherish and to crush

but not a choice to die. That was a given—
part of the package of life. We heard the LORD
say of us, "they might reach out and eat of the tree of life
and live forever."

We didn't.
That choice the LORD took from us
and left us as we were made:
mortals with death in our bones.

END

Dust exploded up between his
Bare toes
Before him dull cows walked
Into the falling sun

Holy the Child[5]

Holy the Hindu, Holy the Jew, Holy the Catholic
Holy the Muslim, Holy the Taoist, Holy the Protestant
Holy the Buddhist, Holy the Santos, Holy the Unbeliever
Holy the believers all, Holy the doubters all—holy.

Holy the infant sucking at dry dugs, Holy the infant fat and full
Holy the urchin, famished and dull, Holy the toddler joyous from hugs
Holy the lonely child, Holy the lonely child, Holy the bony child and
the fat
Holy the smart ones, Holy the strong ones, Holy the strugglers
Holy the strugglers, Holy the genius savant and the child ordinaire
Holy the little ones, Holy the big ones, Holy the brown ones and the black,
beige, purple, yellow, rust, ivory, pink and white. Holy the rainbow of
children
Holy the universe of children. Holy children universal
Holy all children spun from one ur-strand of DNA—one birthing, one child

Holy the bleeding child, the bomb torn child, the child gassed
Holy the child orphaned, motherless, fatherless
Holy the child terrorized by the rumor of war, the rumble of war, war
at fierce roar
Holy the child damaged collaterally, damaged permanently, damaged
mind, body and soul

Holy the child—holy.

---

[5] A homage to Allen Ginsberg's "Foote to *Howl*" through the lens of the "shock
and awe" attack on Baghdad.

The Slaughter of the Innocents

Kindermass 28 December 2012 (Feast of the Holy Innocents).
Sandy Hook School Shooting, December 14, 2012.

It is a hard thing, this season of waiting
Candle light in the midst of darkness
is prologue but hardly bright—
even the joy candle does not
hold back the heavy blackness
that settles in the heart.

There is the baby king in the manger
the horrible Herod on his throne,
lowliness; there are peasants.
The angels do not come to Bethlehem
And the innocents are slaughtered

We must always remember
Between the times
That the innocents are slaughtered

The heart goes from wonder to wondering—
to why?—and to how could!—
if there is love
and justice and righteousness?

Red heat of anger
red eyes
the weeping, disconsolate

Mystery is terribly thick and terribly dark
darker than anything seen through a mirror

Today our eyes are matted in the slick black of coagulated blood
Only four small candles of waiting to give us sight—only three are lit.

At Table

It is hard
to sip
the cup of salvation
after
swallowing
the bread of tears

I Am

The burning bush
That shall not be consumed

The flash of fire
That cannot be extinguished

The blaze of light
That cannot be dimmed

Stronger than death
A raging flame

The burning lips of love

Today

Today I think it is time
to stop the world. Align!
Time to grasp life's start,
to hear again my heart.
Time to suck in cold air
and taste beyond salt tear.
Time to tear open new
Eyes, gain a clear view.
Blue no longer. Red now
like blood splashed on fresh snow.

Time Gently Bends

The sharp edges of life
the nicks and cuts of fortune
the cutting blades of time
bleed us of life
sever us from kin
diminish our power.
drain us of hope.

All flesh pales
shoulders stoop,
skin sags,
joints lock,
bone grates on bone
synapses clot
the present dies
the past retreats
a dullness comes
a darkening . . .
and
"It is finished!"

We who were buried in living water
are also buried corruptible

—Ashes to dust, dirt to dirt—

Walk with me past the grave's edge
beyond the sharp edges

past the nicks and cuts
and whirling blades
beyond the body corruptible
come to that edge with me
where time gently bends

Does Life Die

So, here's the question:
If life ends, and it does,
does it die?
Can the holy breath of beginnings end?
Can death extinguish it—
the breath that forms us,
the informs us, and
that shall,
in the blast of the trumpet
transform us.
Can that breath die?

Life Abundant

To rot in the earth lightly wrapped
or join those who wander the shadow realm
is much preferred to eternal rest.

I have rested best when sleep was deep
when my mind wore an easy yoke,
an unbearable lightness,
after a day of exhilarating mind-work
or exhaustion from the sweat of my brow

Eternal rest lacks even
the motion of disintegrating flesh,
lacks the communion of feeding larva,
is in all ways deader than death

Let us die into usefulness,
animate,
greening the grass,
rising to the purpose of justice,
establishing right(eous)ness,
creating wholeness,
bringing wellness—
dying as life, for life, to life
busy, thrumming abundant, eternal life.

Acknowledgments

Day Spring (Episcopal Diocese WV Vol. 104, No.2 2005): "The Agony and the Ecstasy"

Harbinger (Bethany College WV): "The Ache of It," "At Table," "Ben Hur Nursing Home," "Days of Death and Dying," "End," "Fermenting Joy," "Glass Dancing," "Holy the Child," "4-H Club Pest Drive," "Hydrangeas and Stuffed Shirts," "It Wasn't Like That," "Mirror, Mirror," "On the Fly" ("Catch and Release"), "Peanut Butter Days," "The Shine of It," "The Slaughter of the Innocent."

Laurel Review: "Kingfisher, Vol. 16, No.2 Summer, 1982" "The Visitation Vol. 20, No 1 and 2, Summer 1987"

Outscape. Writings on Fences and Frontiers (2008): "Celtic Knot." (see also *Harbinger*)

Pegasus Review November-December 2000: "Beyond Belief," "Upon a Slender Stalk"

The Southern Poetry Anthology. Volume III: Contemporary Appalachia (2010). "Get You Up To The High Mountain."

I begin by thanking my middle school teacher whose name I do not recall. I shall call her Ms. Fowler and note the she charged me with plagiarizing a poem assigned for her class. She insisted a person my age could not write such a poem. I was dragged to the principal's office, my parents were called, and I was charged with cheating and lying. She could offer nothing more than her certain hunch and my parents testified to watching me scribble out the lines. I was confirmed as a true scribbler. Perhaps this volume derives from that event.

Many thanks to the many editors of Harbinger, Bethany College's literary magazine. Most of my poems first appeared there. Between the demands of teaching and scholarship, I did not work the "little magazines" or seek out chap book publication. But Harbinger gave me an audience and an incentive to write. Thanks one and all!

Also a big thank you to the students who read poetry deeply and passionately in many a course, and to those with whom I honed my craft and theirs as we wrote poetry together in a variety of courses and workshops. Many of you have launched well beyond your teacher.

Now to give thanks: Julie Bloemke and Marc Harshman, thanks for the sharp critical eyes and the wonderful support (*il miglior fabro*); thanks Bethany College students who loved literature with me and who shared their poems and stories in workshops, with a special nod to the editors of *Harbinger*; thanks also to the many joined me in worship, prayer and theological reflection, special thanks to the students at Buffalo Seminary and to Thad Allen and Jim Trader who made the Seminary possible, and to David Chafin who edited several volumes of Advent and Lenten meditations, thanks to Ron Walden and Beth Fletcher for the beautiful flowers on the cover and an ever more beautiful friendship, and to Jeffrey and Nancy Seglin who open arms and open house have kept the juices flowing. Finally, and most especially, thanks to Carol, Becca, Mike, Althea and Grey the Cat, who grant me quiet time and let me play with words and who love the grumpy bear.

About the Author

Larry Grimes is Professor Emeritus of English in the Gresham Chair for Humanities at Bethany College (WV) where he was Department Chair for 25 years. He also served as Dean of Arts and Sciences and Vice President and Dean of the Faculty. He is the author of The Religious Design of Hemingway's Early Fiction and, with Bickford Sylvester, editor of Hemingway, Cuba, and the Cuban Works, and with Bickford Sylvester and Peter Hays, author of The Old Man and the Sea. for the Kent State University Press. A founding member of the Hemingway Society, he has served on the Hemingway Society Board and is, presently, Director of the International Hemingway Conference scheduled for July 2022 in Sheridan, Wyoming and Cooke City, Montana.

In addition to his several essays on Hemingway, he has published essays on crime fiction, the films of Alfred Hitchcock and the Coen Brothers, and is completing a collection of poems. In his spare time, he makes a drinkable cabernet sauvignon and teases trout every chance he can get.

CPSIA information can be obtained
at www.ICGtesting.com
Printed in the USA
LVHW091551280222
712179LV00006BB/239

9 781665 548069